Our World in Color
People of the World

Our World in Color

People of the World

by Arlene Rourke

Silver Press, Inc.
Windermere, Florida 32786

Published by Silver Press, Inc.
Windermere, Florida, 32786
Copyright 1981 Silver Press, Inc.
Copyright The Hamlyn Publishing Group
Limited 1979

Library of Congress Cataloging in Publication Data

Rourke, Arlene, 1944-
  People of the world.

  (Our world in color)
  For grades 5-8.
  Summary: Photographs and brief text introduce
the various ways people dress, work, live, go to
school, play, and travel throughout the world.
  1. Manners and customs—Juvenile literature.
[1. Manners and customs] I. Title.
GT85.R68   390   81-5820
ISBN 0-86593-012-0   AACR2

People of the World

People of the world wear different clothes.

Sometimes they wear national costumes, the special clothes of their country.

The three girls are from France. Do you like their costumes?

The Japanese girl below is dressed in a special robe called a kimono. She carries a pretty umbrella.

Here are a mother and baby from Nigeria. The mother's dress is so big she can carry her baby in it.

The women in the red dresses are from Iran.

The dancers are from Kenya. They are wearing feathers in their hair.

Do you like their big drums?

Sometimes people pray in special clothes.

The girls praying by the river are from Japan. They are wearing kimonos.

This monk from Ethiopia wears a white robe and takes off his shoes when he prays.

Below is a church in Kenya. Can you see the bishop in his hat?

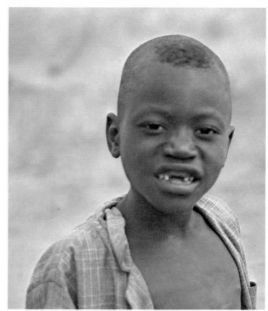

Some countries are hot and some are cold.
Children who live in cold countries need to wear heavy clothes and boots to stay warm when they go outside.
Children in warm areas do not need to wear many clothes.
Do you know where these children live?
Is it hot or cold where you live?

Different people in the world do different jobs.

All these men are fishermen. They are catching fish for people to eat.

The fishermen in the yellow coats are from New England. They are fishing in the sea.

The man below is fishing in a lake in Africa. He is catching big fish.

These people are working to get food.

The man standing on a ladder is picking peppers in Borneo. The man with the big pan lives in France. He is crushing grapes to make wine.

The women working in the water are planting rice in Malaysia. Below two African men are plowing the land so they can plant seeds.

Some people work with animals.

These men in South America have caught a steer. They are trimming its long horns.

Below is a man from Australia. His job is to cut wool off sheep.

The wool will be used to make cloth. The sheep will soon grow another coat.

Here are two women working with wool to make cloth. The wool has been made into yarn and dyed pretty colors.

The old woman is from Nepal. She is weaving yarn on a small loom in her lap.

The young woman is from Scotland. She is working on a big loom inside a factory.

People live in different ways.

These two men live in Australia. They hunt and fish for food. They are called nomads because they do not stay in one place for very long.

Below is a large family from the desert in Tunisia. They have put up a tent to live in.

Many people live in cities.

In the city of Rouen, France, people sell flowers in the street.

Below is London, a very large city in England. Can you see the big red buses?

On the next page is Tokyo, Japan.

The people below live in a city in Burma. They are washing in a river. Can you see their house behind them?

Wherever they live, children want to learn.

These Japanese girls are going to school. They are wearing uniforms, clothes that are just alike.

Some schools are held outdoors.

These children live in India.

They sit on the ground while they study. One boy is standing up to read his lesson.

The school below is an indoor school. It is in Nigeria. The children are working at their desks.

Are these schools like yours? How are they different?

These Afghanistan children are studying their lessons outdoors.

In a Chinese school a girl is learning about numbers. Can you see the Chinese letters?

The American children below are having a geography lesson. They are studying the globe.

People of the world like to enjoy themselves.

Two boys from Kashmir are dancing to the beat of their drums.

The three children playing on the beach are from Spain. Do you think the weather is warm there?

What might the children below be laughing at?

Grown-ups enjoy playing, too.

The men dressed in white are playing a game called cricket. Below them are a tennis player and a gymnast.

People in many countries like to ice skate. These people are skating in New York City.

Some people like to play dangerous games.
Football players wear helmets and padding so
they won't hurt themselves.

The cowboy is trying to see how long he can
ride a bull. The Spanish man is using a red
cloak to tease a bull.

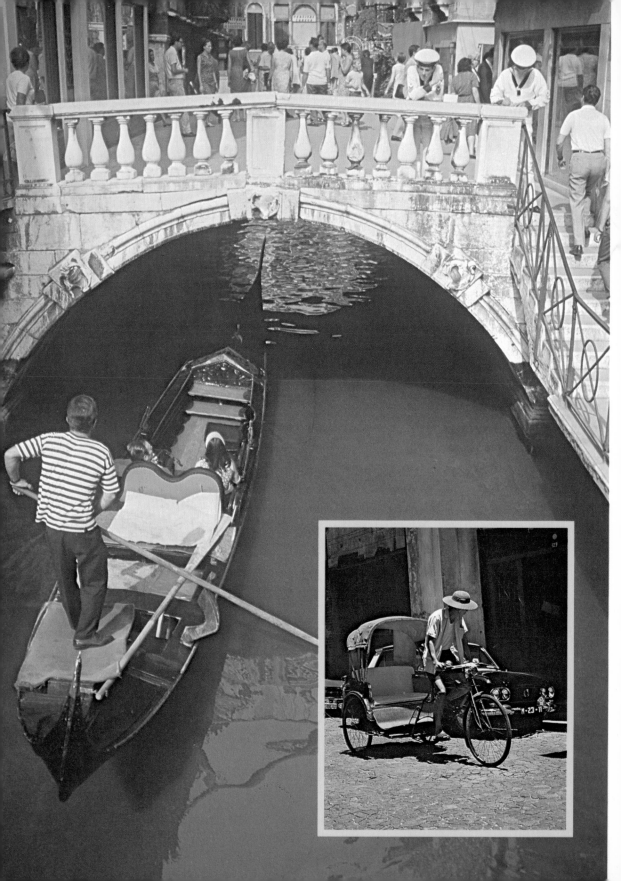

People of the world travel in different ways.

The man in the long boat lives in Venice, Italy. His boat is called a gondola.

The man pulling the cart with his bicycle lives in China. Would you like to ride with him?

The woman below lives in Spain. She has cattle to pull her cart.

In Hong Kong people can travel in boats like those in the small picture on the next page.

People in India sometimes travel in a cart called a rickshaw. A man pulls the rickshaw along the road.

The cart below is in Italy. It is pulled by a horse. Can you see cars in the picture, too?

Could you carry your food on your head like these African Women?

Below is a man from Singapore selling fruits and vegetables. His daughter is helping.

The top picture on the next page shows a market in Morocco.

The man from Pakistan in the bottom picture has lots of food to sell.

This little boy from Singapore is eating his dinner. Can you see the rice on his plate?

The men in the red hats are from Holland. They are carrying big yellow cheeses.

This woman is buying a yellow melon at a market.

Which places in this book would you like to see? Which people would you like to visit?